Published by The Child's World®
1980 Lookout Drive • Mankato, MN 56003-1705
800-599-READ • www.childsworld.com

ACKNOWLEDGMENTS
The Child's World®: Mary Berendes, Publishing Director
The Design Lab: Design
Jody Jensen Shaffer: Editing
Pamela J. Mitsakos: Photo Research

PHOTO CREDITS
CEFutcher/iStock.com: 16; cobalt/Shutterstock.com: 5; Dmitry Naumov/
iStock.com: 22; Feverpitch Photography/iStock.com: 21; GlobalStock/
iStock.com: 18; Massonstock/iStock.com: 6; MaszaS/Shutterstock.com:
cover, 1; Max Topchii/Shutterstock.com: 13; RoyvanHuffelen/iStock.com:
10; SeaHorseTwo/iStock.com: 9; zvonko1959/iStock.com: 14

ISBN 9781626870260
LCCN 2013947394

Printed in the United States of America in Mankato, Minnesota.
September 2014
PA02249

ABOUT THE AUTHORS

Cynthia Amoroso has worked as an elementary school teacher and a high school English teacher. Writing children's books is another way for her to share her passion for the written word.

Robert B. Noyed has worked as a newspaper reporter and in the communications department for a Minnesota school district. He enjoys the challenge and accomplishment of writing children's books.

Summer

BY CYNTHIA AMOROSO AND ROBERT B. NOYED

Summer is here! Summer is one of the four seasons. It comes after spring and before fall.

Summer is the third season of the year.

Summer is the hottest season.
Many of the days are sunny,
too. The sun shines late into
the evening.

Sunglasses protect your eyes from the bright summer sun.

Sometimes there are strong storms during summer. Thunder, lightning, and heavy rain are common during this time of year. Some storms might have tornadoes.

Summer storms can sometimes be dangerous.

The rain and sun help plants grow. Trees and bushes are full of leaves. Flowers bloom and show their many colors.

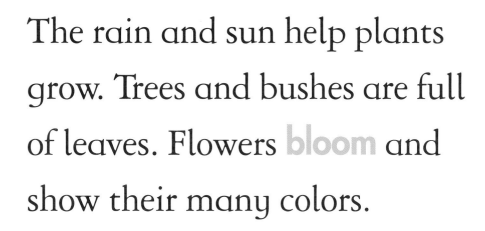

Wildflowers come in many different colors.

Many people take care of gardens in the summer. They grow tomatoes, beans, peas, carrots, and other vegetables. Many berries are ready to pick in the summer.

This girl grew tomatoes and squash in her garden.

Bees are very busy in the summer. They buzz from flower to flower. They make honey in their hives.

This honeybee is sitting on a dandelion.

Summer is a busy time. People like to go swimming, boating, and fishing. Many people go on vacations in the summer.

Always wear your lifejacket when boating.

Camping is great in the summer, too. Campers roast hot dogs and marshmallows over campfires.

Camping can be a lot of fun!

Many people enjoy summer picnics with family and friends. There are many parades that are fun to watch.

Picnics are a fun way to enjoy the outdoors.

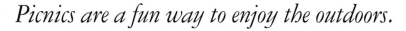

There are lots of things to do
in the summer. Go outside
and enjoy the sunny weather!

The beach is a great place to spend a summer day.

Glossary

bloom (BLOOM): When flowers open up, they bloom. most flowers bloom in the spring and summer.

hives (HYVZ): Hives are where bees live. Bees make honey in hives.

parades (puh-RAYDZ): Parades are when people march for holidays. The Fourth of July has lots of parades.

roast (ROHST): If people roast something, they cook it. Hot dogs can roast over a campfire.

seasons (SEE-zinz): Seasons are the four parts of the year. The four seasons are winter, spring, summer, and fall.

vacations (vay-KAY-shunz): Vacations are time off from work or school to rest or to travel. Many families take vacations in the summer.

To Find Out More

Books

Branley, Franklyn M. *Sunshine Makes the Seasons*. New York: HarperCollins, 2005.

Latta, Sara. *Why Is It Summer?* Berkeley Heights, NJ: Enslow Publishers, 2012.

Rockwell, Anne. *Four Seasons Make a Year*. New York: Walker & Co., 2004.

Web Sites

Visit our Web site for links about summer: *childsworld.com/links*

Note to Parents, Teachers, and Librarians: We routinely verify our Web links to make sure they are safe and active sites. So encourage your readers to check them out!

Index